DOWN FROM COLONIALISM

MEXICO'S

NINETEENTH CENTURY CRISIS

View of the Zocalo, the plaza mayor *of Mexico City*

JAIME E. RODRIGUEZ O.

Down From Colonialism

With an introduction by
Roberto Moreno de los Arcos

CHICANO STUDIES RESEARCH CENTER PUBLICATIONS

UNIVERSITY OF CALIFORNIA

LOS ANGELES

Library of Congress Cataloging in Publication Data

Rodríguez O., Jaime E., 1940-
  Down from colonialism.

  (Popular series / Chicano Studies Research Center Publications; no. 3)
    Includes bibliographical references.
    1. Mexico—Economic conditions—19th century.
    2. Mexico—Politics and government—19th century.
    3. Mexico—History—Spanish colony, 1540-1810.
    I. Title.   II. Series: Popular series (University of California, Los Angeles. Chicano Studies Research Center. Publications); no. 3

  HC135.R48   1983   330.972   83-14331
  ISBN 0-89551-064-2

Chicano Studies Research Center Publications

Popular Series No. 3

Publications Coordinator: Oscar R. Martí, Ph.D.
Editorial Assistants:
Mr. Roberto R. Calderón, M.A.
Ms. Alicia Rodríguez, M.F.A.

© 1983 by the Regents of the University of California and the Chicano Studies Research Center, University of California, Los Angeles. All rights reserved. This is a redesigned and slightly revised version of a lecture first published in 1981 under the same title by the Regents of the University of California. Printed with permission of the author. The introduction by Roberto Moreno de los Arcos is published here for the first time.

Composition: Freedmen's Organization of Los Angeles
Design: Serena Sharp / Los Angeles Publication Design
Produced by UCLA Publication Services Department

Printed in the United States of America.

A mi madre
María Beatríz Ordoñez

Contents

Preface xi

Introduction xvii

Acknowledgments xxiii

Down from Colonialism
Mexico's Nineteenth Century Crisis 1

Notes 35

Bibliography 43

New Spain's maximum claims to North America, 1802.

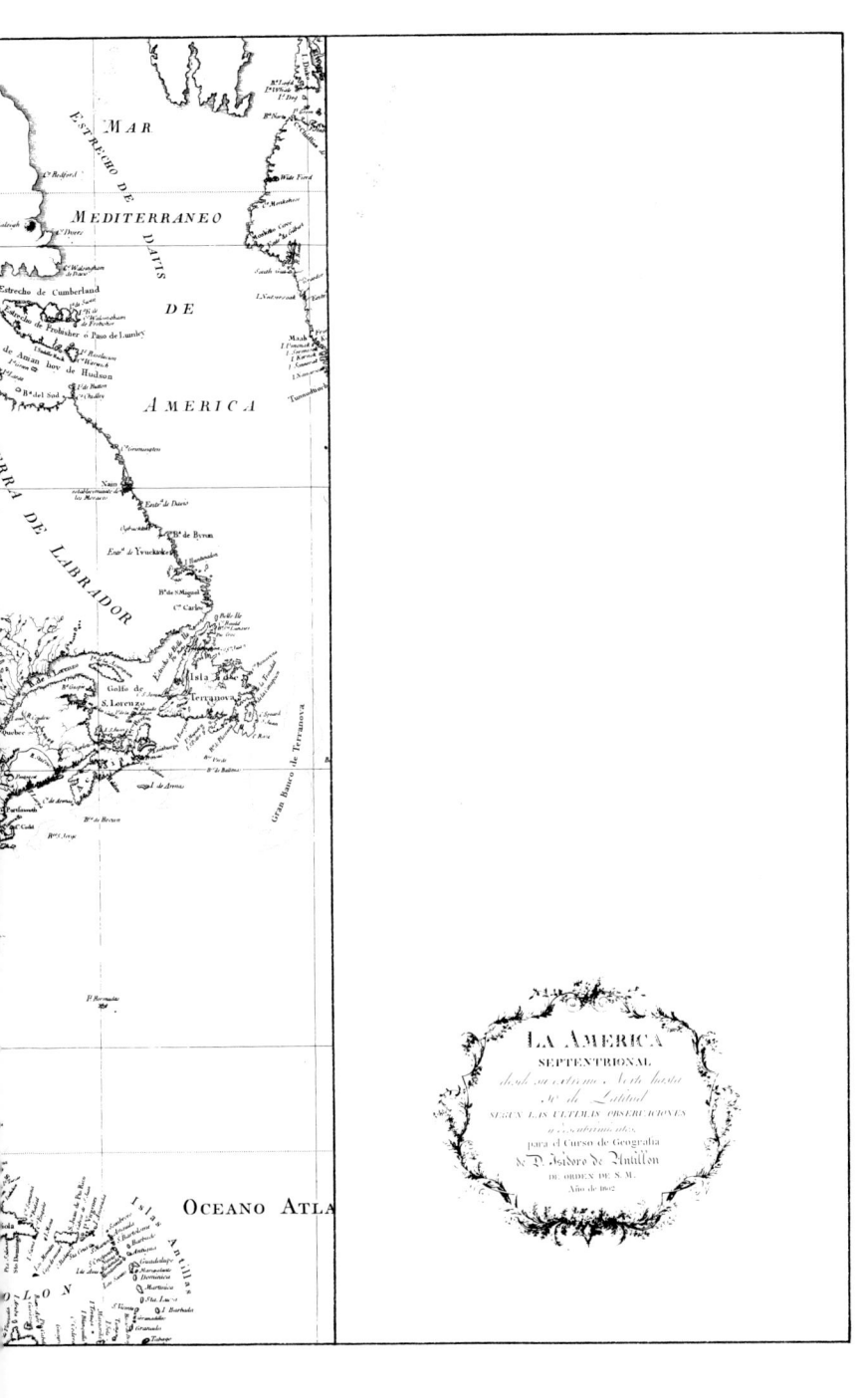

Preface

This essay is an expanded and revised version of the *Distinguished Faculty Lecture* which Professor Jaime E. Rodríguez O. delivered at the University of California, Irvine on May 28, 1980.

The University of California's Distinguished Faculty Lectureship Award, given each year by the Academic Senate, is the highest award University of California faculty members can receive from their colleagues. The honor is conferred on faculty who have made significant contributions to knowledge through distinguished research and who have brought to themselves and to the University national and international recognition. The Distinguished Faculty Lectureship Award is deeply rooted in the University's tradition of excellence and demonstrates the high caliber of University of California faculty. Although there are many honors for outstanding scholarship, recognition by one's peers, which the Distinguished Faculty Lectureship Award accords, has special significance that accompanies no other honor.

Jaime E. Rodríguez O., internationally recognized for his research on Latin American history, was named by the Irvine Division of the Academic Senate as co-recipient of the 1980 Distinguished Faculty Lectureship Award. Professor Rodríguez is a member of the Department of History at the University of California, Irvine, and is Dean of the Division of Graduate Studies and Research.

Professor Rodríguez's work seeks to explain Spanish America's failure to modernize in the early nineteenth century. At the time Western Europe and the United States were being transformed into modern industrial societies, the newly independent nations of Spanish America were crippled by economic depression and extreme political instability. Scholars have generally argued that this failure to modernize stemmed from the feudal Spanish colonial structure which did not prepare Spanish Americans for self government. According to this view, after independence Spanish American leaders rejected colonial tradition and adopted foreign systems of government unsuited to their nations' needs, causing Spanish America's nineteenth century crisis. After examining the problems of nation building in Spanish America, Professor Rodríguez concluded that the traditional explanations were wrong. In a series of studies, he showed that independence was not a sharp break with the past and that Spanish American leaders had not blindly accepted alien forms of government. These arguments are developed extensively in two books, *Estudios sobre Vicente Rocafuerte* (Guayaquil, 1975) and *The Emergence of Spanish America* (Berkeley & Los Angeles, 1975), which demonstrate the continuity of the Spanish and Spanish American reform tradition and its influence upon the leaders of the new countries.

Although the nineteenth century "failure" could no longer be attributed to a rejection of Spanish traditions, many scholars maintained that the Spanish heritage was negative and that Spanish America's underdevelopment originated in the colonial epoch when neofeudal institutions and practices were established. Professor Rodríguez and Professor Colin M. MacLachlan, of Tulane University, undertook an exhaustive study of Mexico's colonial experience in order to test the validity of the neo-feudal theses. They selected Mexico for study because it was colonial Spanish America's largest, most populous, and most important region. The research presented major difficulties because significant aspects of Mexico's history remained unstudied, necessitating extensive investigation in Mexican archives. The results of Rodríguez's and MachLachlan's work appear in a volume entitled *The Forging of the Cosmic Race: A Reinterpretation of Colonial Mexico* (Berkeley and Los Angeles, 1980) which received the Hubert Herring Memorial Award in 1980. The authors argue that colonial Mexico was not a feudal but a capitalist society; that the region developed a complex, balanced, and integrated economy which transformed it into the most dynamic part of the Spanish empire; and that it was one of the few regions of the world where racial and cultural intermingling created a new society, a *cosmic race*, to use José Vasconcelos's evocative phrase.

Having examined and rejected the two major theses advanced to explain Spanish America's nineteenth century "failure," Professor Rodríguez concluded that an adequate explanation must be sought in the post-independence period. He is presently engaged in two studies of the epoch: an analysis of Mexico's early nineteenth century economy to explain why one of the Western Hemisphere's most prosperous areas plunged into a prolonged economic depression in the first half of the nineteenth century, and a second work, a study of Quito, Ecuador during the years 1750–1850, to examine the way in which a peripheral area of Spanish America made the transition from colony to independence. These studies will investigate those local factors which mitigated or intensified the crisis, as well as supply data for a comparative analysis of the broader problem of Spanish America's nineteenth century crisis.

Professor Rodríguez received his Ph.D. from the University of Texas at Austin in 1970. From 1969 to 1973, he was on the faculty of California State University, Long Beach. In 1973, he joined the Department of History at the University of California, Irvine. He served as Associate Dean of Humanities in 1979 and became Graduate and Research Dean in 1980.

Professor Rodríguez's scholarly contributions have received wide recognition. His honors include an Organization of American States Fellowship, a Foreign Area Fellowship, a Social Science Research Council Fellowship, a Mellon Foundation Fellowship, a Fullbright Research Fellowship, and corresponding memberships in the National Academy of History of Ecuador and the Centro de Estudios Históricos del Guayas. In 1980, he was named a Fellow of the Institute of Historical Research of the National Autonomous University of Mexico. Professor Rodríguez is the only historian to have been elected Chair to two regional committees of the conference on Latin American History: the Andean Studies Committee in 1976 and the Mexican Studies Committee in 1979–1980. He served as President of the Pacific Coast Council of Latin American Studies in 1979–80. Professor

Rodríguez is a member of the American Historical Association, the Conference on Latin American History, the Congress of Mexican and North American Historians, the Latin American Studies Association, the Pacific Coast Council of Latin American Studies, and the National Chicano Council on Higher Education.

Roberto Moreno de los Arcos, the Director of the Institute of Historical Research at the National Autonomous University of Mexico, is a leading expert in the history of science, particularly in the eighteenth century. He has published many articles and books in Mexico, Spain, France, and the United States. Among his best known works are: Joaquín Velázquez de León y sus trabajos científicos sobre el Valle de México *(Mexico, 1977);* La polémica del darwinismo en México *(Mexico, 1983); and* Obras completas de José Antonio Alzate *(Mexico, 1980–). He is currently completing a three-volume study of the urban development of Mexico City. Professor Moreno de los Arcos' scholarly contributions have received wide recognition. He is one of 36 members of the National Academy of the Language of Mexico; he is one of 24 members of the National Academy of History of Mexico; and he is a corresponding member of the Royal Academy of History of Spain. In 1981, he was awarded the National Prize for Social Science by the National Academy of Science of Mexico. In October, 1982, the Pacific Coast Council on Latin American Studies bestowed its Distinguished Scholar Award upon Prof. Moreno de los Arcos in recognition of his contribution to the field. He was recently awarded a John Simon Guggenheim Memorial Foundation grant to complete his study of Mexico City.*

Introduction

The historian's task is of necesity ample and varied, especially in countries with a rich but not extensively studied past. The historian of Mexico is obliged to fulfill a very extensive role which includes the publication of documents, critical editions, and translations; the preparation of indexes, guides, and catalogs; and the activity which the scholarly world considers the highest task of the professional historian: the research and writing of monographs and interpretative essays.

In reality, history—I am referring to what historians write, rather than the past itself—is an eternal and fascinating Penelope's cloth. It is always necessary to rewrite history. This, of course, is not a historiographical defect, and one should not reach the hasty conclusion that historians whose studies have been superseded did not do their work well or distorted the facts. The more a particular event is studied, the easier it is to develop new themes, broader theses, and critical revisions. The writing of history is also immersed in the historial evolution of societies, and it responds to the concerns which society holds at a particular time. I have always believed that historical truth does not exist and that if it did we would have no way of recognizing it. The theme of historical truth seems like a Gordian knot that has only Alexander's false solution—to sever it. In the real world, the work of professional historians must be judged through other perspectives. In my view, the solution to the problem of historical truth lies in the efficacy of a historical explanation at a given moment and for a sufficiently large social group. That is, history attempts to explain a past phenomenon or process, and it is effective as an explanation to the extent that a single thesis explains more aspects of historical reality and a larger public accepts the interpretation.

Nothing is more difficult in this context than to struggle against prejudices and explanations generally, and on occasion uncritically, accepted. Thus, it is sometimes necessary to challenge the "classical" works of historiography, that body of knowledge which we inherited from our teachers, not to blame them for what they did but to seek new paths for historical inquiry. To propose new—and even provocative—theories is one of the healthiest ways of maintaining the youthfulness of one of our oldest disciplines.

It is with these points in mind that I want to discuss Jaime E. Rodríguez O.'s work as a historian. Professor Rodríguez received solid professional preparation at the University of Texas, where he studied with the outstanding and erudite historian Dr. Nettie Lee Benson. The results of his training may be seen in his many publications—documents, critical editions, translations, and guides, as well as numerous monographs which have appeared in the leading journals in the field. In his first book-length monograph, *The Emergence of Spanish America: Vicente Rocafuerte and Spanish Americanism, 1808–1832* (Berkeley, 1975), Rodríguez presented in an enlightening manner a series of events which we had not understood before. He demonstrated the existence of a phase of the revolutions for Spanish American independence in which important groups of prominent people believed in and worked for the integration of the new nations without rejecting a possible understanding with Spain. This movement, which Rodríguez called *Spanish Americanism*, appears to have convinced many Spanish American leaders that they could obtain *liberty* without necessarily having to achieve *independence*. Rodríguez's book thus presented us with the possibility of revising our ideas about a crucial and painful period in our independence movement.

Working with the distinguished Mexicanist, Colin M. MacLachlan, Rodríguez published an interpretative monograph, *The Forging of the Cosmic Race: A Reinterpretation of Colonial Mexico* (Berkeley, 1980), which will soon appear in Spanish with the title *La forja de la raza cósmica*. I want to emphasize two aspects of the work. First, it is an original contribution based on an exhaustive study of the published literature as well as research in the archives of various countries. Second, it is a landmark in the historiography of colonial Mexico.

Prior to the publication of this work, those three centuries were viewed as an exceedingly obscure and negative age. The non-Spanish literature had continued with the old "Black Legend" of Spanish colonialism, a view which the Spanish American liberals had adopted not only as a defense against attempts to reconquer the area but as an ideology with which to oppose conservatism. The earlier scholarly historiography did not remain uninfluenced by such strong ideological currents. In addition, scholars accepted the mechanical notion that a colony, of necessity, must be worse off than the metropolis. Although it is true that many researchers had already contributed new perspectives about aspects of the colonial epoch, it is clear that a new general interpretation of those three centuries was absolutely necessary. Rodríguez's and MacLachlan's work is precisely that. Their study puts an end to a widely accepted thesis about the colonial period; their work also enables us to initiate new research with approaches that are less biased than the old paradigms. Their work does not postulate truth —that is not possible. It simply proposes a new and enriching approach to Mexico's colonial age which will change the direction of research, despite criticism and disagreements. To perfect, to amplify, or to challenge their study is a fundamental contribution to Mexican historiography.

Rodríguez has continued working intensely in search of a global explanation of Mexico's historical process. It was natural that he would follow *The Forging of the Cosmic Race* with an attempt to understand the causes of Mexico's contemporary situation. That is the purpose of the essay on the nineteenth century crisis for which I am writing these introductory lines. In it Rodríguez asks why, if New Spain at the beginning of the nineteenth century seemed so opulent, did the new Mexican nation not continue to prosper? The reader will find his answer in the pages that follow. What I am interested in highlighting here is the significance of this text within the body of Rodríguez's historical work. This essay is the logical continuation of his earlier studies. It is the confirmation that the process of historical thinking in his previous writings does not follow a meandering course, but that it forms part of a solid and original conception of the entire course of Mexico's history.

The essay on the nineteenth century crisis continues the arguments expressed in the book on colonial Mexico. It is one of the first essays that eschews a detailed account of political events to seek instead the substratum of history. Such an approach was necessary. After a few pioneering works had studied sectors of the nineteenth century economy and society, someone had to analyze the continuities which colonial society had forged in three centuries and their effects on the country after independence. Rodríguez's essay, in this respect, answers the crucial questions: Why did Mexico not recover quickly after independence? Why did it sink into fifty years of economic depression and political disorder? The questions asked by Rodríguez are, in my opinion, an achievement in themselves. The answers he provides are further proof of the thoroughness of his research and the keenness of his perception. As in his earlier works, Rodríguez manages to provide a coherent interpretation of events which earlier had appeared confusing. His approach, to analyze events internal and external to Mexico, is a genuine advance. Reading his essay will arouse new concerns, new doubts, and new questions about the history of Mexico. I can only hope that Rodríguez himself will address these questions in new works that will enrich Mexican history.

> Roberto Moreno de los Arcos
> Institute of Historical Research
> National Autonomous University of Mexico
> March, 1983

Acknowledgments

This essay is an expanded and revised version of the Distinguished Faculty Lecture which I delivered at the University of California, Irvine in May, 1980. In preparing the lecture for publication, I made some stylistic changes, added certain passages, and introduced tables and notes. This required additional research carried out principally at the Bancroft Library of the University of California, Berkeley.

I am both honored and grateful that my colleagues in the Academic Senate selected me to deliver this lecture. I thank the Director of the Institute of Historical Research of the National Autonomous University of Mexico for the opportunity to present a Spanish version of this lecture in Mexico in the Spring of 1981 as well as for the incisive comments he and his colleagues made. I am also grateful to Linda Alexander Rodríguez and William F. Sater for their careful reading of the manuscript. Finally, I thank the Director of the Chicano Studies Research Center for bringing out a new edition of this essay.

Jaime E. Rodríguez O.
Los Angeles
April, 1983

Dancing at a local tavern.

COLONIAL MEXICO (New Spain) was a vast territory characterized by a stable and responsive government, a wealthy and balanced economy, and a multi-racial society which enjoyed considerable social mobility. Yet, by the middle of the nineteenth century, the republic of Mexico not only had lost more than half its territory, but also suffered from extreme political instability, severe economic depression, and both racial as well as class conflict. This lecture will examine Mexico's decline from colonial well-being to republican disaster. Since many today mistakenly consider the colonial era to have been backward, feudal, and exploitative, I shall begin by contrasting New Spain in 1800 with Mexico around 1850.

The Viceroyalty of New Spain was the Western Hemisphere's most imposing political structure at the end of the eighteenth century. Its territory included present-day Mexico, Central America, the Philippines, Cuba, Puerto Rico, Florida, the coastal regions of Alabama and Mississippi, and all the lands west of the Mississippi River, as well as claims to western Canada and Alaska. The heartland of the viceroyalty, however, was a region, about the size of present day Mexico, known as the Kingdom of New Spain. That area, the subject of this lecture, was the richest and most populous part of the viceroyalty.

New Spain's institutions responded well to local needs. Indeed, a notable feature of the colony's government was its legitimacy, derived from the confidence it engendered in all classes and races. Colonial Mexicans normally availed themselves of administrative and legal procedures to obtain relief. Even Indians had sufficient confidence in the legal system to seek redress in the courts where they frequently won their suits because colonial tribunals recognized the validity of native laws and customs. Thus, there was general agreement in New Spain that royal government, both at the local and at the imperial level, served the public interest. This consensus did not mean that all disputes were settled peacefully; violence occasionally erupted. But such outbursts were rare, seeking to remedy specific grievances, not to challenge the colony's political, social, or economic order. To a great extent, this success was due to the fact that New Spain drew upon its domestic elite for guidance; colonial Mexicans generally responded to their country's problems with moderate, rational, and practical solutions.

The colony's great wealth contributed to government stability and to the dynamism of Mexican society. New Spain provided two thirds of the revenue of the Spanish empire. In 1799, this amounted to 20 million pesos, ten million of which was spent for local administration and defense; four million subsidized other areas of the viceroyalty in Central and North America, the Caribbean, and the Philippines; and six million was remitted to the royal treasury in Madrid.

Mine shaft typical of the great ninteenth century silver mines.

TABLE I
Estimates of New Spain's Gross National Product ca. 1800*

Sector	Domestic Consumption		Exports		Total	
	Amount	%	Amount	%	Amount	%
Agriculture	133,782,625	70.5%	4,844,685	15.1%	138,627,310	62.0%
Industry	54,744,047	29.0%	257,264	0.8%	55,001,311	25.0%
Mining	924,259	0.5%	27,026,741	84.1%	27,951,000	13.0%
Total	189,450,931	100.0%	32,128,690	100.0%	221,579,621	100.0%
% of the Economy	86%		14%		100%	

*In pesos.

Source: Calculated from José María Quirós, *Memoria de estatuto* (Veracruz, 1817). Errors in the figures originally published by Quirós have been corrected by Doris M. Ladd, *The Mexican Nobility at Independence* (Austin, 1976), p. 26.

Revenues increased during the next decade, averaging 24 million pesos per year. In 1806, when unusual demands were placed on the Spanish colonies, Mexico raised 39 million pesos, sending 19 million to Spain to help finance the wars in Europe.[1]

The economy of New Spain was healthy, balanced, and, for the most part, functioned independently of the mother country. Although precious metals represented 84% of all exports, the colony did not become a simple mono-producer, as some dependency theorists have suggested. Despite its critical and dynamic character, mining constituted only a minor segment of the colonial economy. In 1800, mining contributed 27.95 million pesos, or 13% of Mexico's annual production, while manufacturing accounted for 55 million, or 25%, and agriculture 138.63 million, or 62%. Mexico's large and diversified internal market consumed 86% of all national production, as table I shows.

The silver mines, however, served as engines of economic growth, encouraging the expansion of agriculture, commerce, and manufacturing. Mexico was the world's principal supplier of silver throughout the colonial period. During the years 1780–1810, New Spain produced an average of 24 million pesos of silver annually.[2] Although precise figures on production are not available, one can estimate silver output by examining coinage, which accounted for more than 95% of the silver mined in Mexico.

Mining required investment on a vast scale. The cost of labor, machinery, and supplies necessary for the largest operations was staggering. In the 1780s, for example, Antonio de Obregón borrowed capital from local merchants to rework old sixteenth century diggings in Guanajuato. After

TABLE II
Coinage of Silver in Mexico, 1796–1825

Year	Millions of Pesos	Year	Millions of Pesos
1796[a]	24.4	1811[c,e]	10.1
1797[a]	24.1	1812[c,e]	7.7
1798[a]	23.0	1813[c,e]	9.8
1799[a]	21.1	1814[d,e]	10.1
1800[a]	17.9	1815[d,e]	8.3
1801[a]	16.0	1816[c,e]	9.6
1802[a]	18.0	1817[c,e]	9.1
1803[a]	22.5	1818[d,e]	12.6
1804[a]	26.1	1819[c]	12.8
1805[a]	25.8	1820[c]	10.8
1806[a]	23.4	1821[d,e]	7.6
1807[a]	20.7	1822[d]	10.4
1808[a]	20.5	1823[d]	10.8
1809[a]	24.7	1824[d]	9.0
1810[b]	18.0	1825[d]	8.3

Notes: [a]Mint of Mexico.
[b]Mints of Mexico and Zacatecas.
[c]Mints of Mexico, Zacatecas, and Durango.
[d]Mints of Mexico, Zacatecas, Durango, and Guadalajara.
[e]During the war years, the mints of Guadalajara and Durango failed to make annual reports, but instead reported for periods of time varying from 6 to 45 months. Since it was impossible to disaggregate those numbers, monthly averages were calculated and multiplied by 12 to obtain yearly figures. Although this approach introduces a degree of error, nevertheless the figures presented in the table are sound estimates of silver coinage for the period.

Source: Calculated from the annual reports of the mints of Mexico City, Guadalajara, Durango, and Zacatecas which are reproduced in Ward, *Mexico*, 1:386–391.

spending over two million pesos to sink some of the deepest mine shafts in existence, his mines produced silver valued at 30.9 million pesos from 1788 to 1809. In just one year, 1791, his mine yielded as much silver as the entire Viceroyalty of Peru.[3] When considering the magnitude of the sums involved in this venture, one should keep in mind that in 1800, the per capita income of England, the most advanced nation in the world, equalled 196 pesos a year.[4] Obregón's impressive achievement depended entirely on local resources. In studying this and other eighteenth century Mexican ventures, one is struck by the high level of capital formation, technological innovation, entrepreneurial spirit, and managerial skills possessed by Mexicans.

A brief comparison with the United States highlights the nature of Mexico's economy in 1800. The per capita income for New Spain was about 116 pesos a year compared with 165 pesos for the United States. The value of Mexican and U.S. exports was the same, about 20 million pesos.[5] Both countries were predominantly agricultural, but Mexico possessed a much larger industrial sector, principally in mining and textile manufacturing.

Other aspects of life in the neighboring regions provide an interesting contrast. In 1800, the United States had a population of six million people while Mexico's inhabitants numbered about four million. The U.S. was overwhelmingly rural while Mexico, although rural, had several of the largest cities in the continent. The principal urban centers of the United States—New York with 60,000 people, Philadelphia with 41,000, and Boston with 25,000—did not compare with the leading cities in New Spain—Mexico City with 150,000 inhabitants, Guanajuato with 60,000, Querétaro with 50,000, Puebla with 40,000, and Zacatecas with 30,000.

Colonial Mexico also differed from the U.S. in its racial composition and in the higher degree of mobility enjoyed by its people. Europeans constituted the majority of the United States' population, with Blacks and Indians forming significant minorities. Whites, however, dominated the political and economic structure of the country, limiting social mobility to members of their race. In contrast, the Mexican census of 1793 indicated that there were approximately 8,000 Europeans, that is, persons born in the Old World; about 700,000 *criollos*—a group considered white but which, in fact, included a majority of people of mixed ancestry who claimed white status by virtue of education and wealth; some 420,000 *mestizos*—individuals of mixed Indian and Spanish origin, but also including acculturated Indians who passed for mestizos; 360,000 *mulatos*; 6,000 Blacks; and 2,300,000 Indians.[6] The Indian enumeration includes more than a million who were acculturated and who could, in essence, be considered mestizos. Unfortunately for the historian, the census failed to enumerate Asians, making it impossible to know their true numbers. Perhaps 100,000 Asians immigrated to Mexico during the colonial period. By 1800 they, like the countless Africans brought to the colony, had entered the racially mixed population. Thus Mexico, unlike its northern counterpart, had a multiracial society integrated through miscegenation.

Economic, rather than racial, factors constituted the main determinants of social status. While colonial Mexicans regarded being white as a positive characteristic, the records of New Spain provide numerous examples of upwardly mobile people of color who attained elite status by making money and then claiming to be white. Indeed, in the eighteenth century, there were so many claimants to white status that in return for a sum of money, the king granted his American subjects a certificate of whiteness, a *Cédula de Gracias al Sacar*. But in New Spain, it was better to be rich than white; rich mestizos and mulattos often hired poor white immigrants from Spain as servants.[7]

Eighteenth century Mexico can be described as a wealthy, capitalist society whose economy was characterized by private ownership of the means of production, by profit-oriented entrepreneurs, by a free wage labor force, and by the exchange of capital, labor, goods, and services in a free market. While there were some limits on the mobility of these economic factors, present research indicates that these restrictions posed no greater obstacles than those existing in eighteenth century England and the United States.

The contrast between New Spain and republican Mexico in 1850 was enormous. The wars of independence and the chaos that followed ruined the nation's economy and destroyed the legitimacy of its institutions. Between 1821 and 1850, only one president, Guadalupe Victoria (1824–1828), completed his term of office. His success is primarily attributable to the two large foreign loans negotiated in 1824 and 1825 which gave his administration financial latitude. During the next twenty years, the Republic endured three constitutions, twenty governments, and more than 100 cabinets. As succeeding administrations proved unable to maintain order and protect lives and property, the country sank into anarchy. Fear and uncertainty became commonplace. Ex-soldiers-turned-bandits infested the highways, obstructing commerce and threatening small towns. These, and other manifestations of social dissolution, contributed to Mexico's instability. The situation worsened when political conflict degenerated into civil war in 1834.

An urban market.

TABLE III
Government Revenue for Selected Years, 1823–1850

Year[1]	Income[2]
1823	5,409,722
1824	8,452,828
1825[a]	9,720,771
1826[b]	13,848,257
1827	14,192,132
1828	11,640,737
1829	12,815,009
1830	12,200,020
1831	17,256,882
1832	16,375,960
1834	19,798,464
1836	26,478,509
1837	18,477,979
1838	15,037,038
1839	27,518,577
1840	19,858,472
1841	21,273,477
1842	26,683,696
1843	29,323,423
1844	25,905,348
1849[c]	23,460,820
1850	16,765,762

Notes: [1]Year runs from July through June unless noted. For example, 1827 included income for period July 1826–June 1827.
[2]Net income in pesos.
[a]January 1825–August 1825.
[b]September 1825–June 1826.
[c]January 1848–June 1849.

Source: These figures were calculated from data in the reports of the Minister of Treasury for the period 1823–1850. México, Secretaría de Hacienda, *Memoria, 1823–1850*.

Large sections of the country were ravaged as federalists and centralists, liberals and conservatives fought for political control. During 1835–1845, secessionists established the republics of Yucatán, Texas, and the Río Grande, but only Texas managed to consolidate its independence. The other regions, however, maintained their autonomy, if not their independence from the national government, by force of arms.[8]

The country's political instability made Mexico easy prey to foreign aggressors. The Republic endured invasions by Spain in 1829, France in 1838, the United States in 1847, and England, Spain, and France in 1861. The nation's disintegration prompted foreign exponents of racial superiority, among them Karl Marx, to hope that "the energetic Yankees" would overwhelm and replace the "lazy" and "degenerate" Mexicans who were incapable of progress.[9] By 1850, many Mexicans feared that their nation would cease to exist; the country had lost more than half its territory and national regeneration seemed unattainable.

During these years, government revenue dropped from an 1806 high of 39 million pesos to a low of 5.4 million in 1823. In the last two decades of the colonial period, government income had averaged 24 million pesos annually compared to 12.2 million in the Republic's first decade. The average revenue increased in 1834–1844 to 23 million pesos a year, but not until the 1880s did collections surpass late colonial averages.

The decline in government income reflected Mexico's post-independence economic depression. Mining provides a graphic example of this crisis. Mineral production fell from an annual average of 25 million pesos in the late colonial period to a low of 6.5 million in 1819, averaging 11 million

TABLE IV
Mexican Silver Production, 1825–1849

Years	Five year annual average in millions of pesos
1825–29	9.2
1830–34	11.3
1835–39	11.5
1840–44	12.4
1845–49	15.6

Sources: Calculated from A. Soetbeer, *Edelmetall-produktion un werthverhältniss zwischen gold und silver* (Gotha, 1874), p. 55; Miguel Lerdo de Tejada, *Comercio exterior de México desde la Conquista hasta hoy.* 2nd ed. (Mexico, 1967).

a year for the next four decades. This dramatic decline was due to decreased production, not to a drop in the price of silver. In 1801–1810, New Spain extracted 5.5 million kilograms, while in 1821–30, Mexican silver production had fallen to 2.6 million kilograms.[10]

Silver output did not equal late colonial production averages until the 1880s. Other sectors experienced similar dislocations. Exports fell from 20 million pesos in 1800 to 5 million in 1825, and averaged 9.5 million for the next three decades.[11]

While Mexico declined and then stagnated, the United States and Western Europe experienced rapid population increase and economic growth. In 1800, New Spain, like the United States, had a dynamic, expanding economy, but during the next fifty years, Mexico fell dramatically behind. The Republic grew to eight million while the population of the United States expanded to 23 million. Mexico's per capita income fell from 116 pesos at the end of the colonial period to 56 pesos a year in 1845, while U.S. per capita income more than doubled. Thus, Mexicans who had earned 70% of U.S. per capita income in 1800 were reduced to 14% in 1845. Even more significant, Mexican output which had equaled 51% of U.S. GNP in 1800 declined to only 8% in 1845.[12] In contrast to the capitalist, market-oriented, free-wage labor economy of the eighteenth century, mid-nineteenth century Mexico must be characterized as having a dual economy: a market oriented sector remained, but it encompassed only some areas, such as Mexico City and the few remaining large provincial cities; most of the country had retreated into self-sufficiency.[13] Ironically, Mexico in 1850 possessed the sort of society and economy which many today mistakenly believe to have characterized colonial Mexico.

The startling contrast between colonial prosperity and order, and republican poverty and disorder defies easy explanations. It is a paradox which can be understood if one realizes that New Spain developed a costly and complex, but extremely fragile, infrastructure in a land that is both poor and harsh. Mexico, a country with limited natural resources, has considerable natural obstacles to national development and integration. Climatic variations that bridge the extremes of stifling heat on the coast to the chilling cold of the mountains pose a severe threat to people and crops. The northern third of the nation is a desert while rain forests cover large areas of the south. Fifty percent of Mexico suffers from a perpetual scarcity of water; only thirteen percent of the country enjoys sufficient rainfall to sustain crops without irrigation. The richest soil often lacks water. Most of the countryside must cope with intermittent drought followed by torrential rains which destroy rather than nourish the land. Less than ten percent of Mexico is arable without extensive man-made improvements. But even with such improvements, the arable soil increases to only about 15% of the nation's territory, an area equal to the arable land in the state of Kansas.[14] Thus, Mexico is impoverished in the most important resource known to man, agricultural land.

Topography is a major barrier to the use of the nation's limited natural resources. Great mountain ranges dominate the landscape. Deep gorges and huge canyons scar Mexico, isolating some of its most productive lands in high mountain valleys. Since the country has no navigable rivers, transportation and communications are restricted to land routes, which are universally expensive when compared to water transport. It was prohibitive in Mexico, as elsewhere, to move cheap bulky products long distances overland. The country's rugged topography, which increased the difficulty and cost of building and maintaining land routes, magnified this general limitation on interregional exchanges. Since many of the roads passed through mountainous terrain and were subject to destruction by floods, earthquakes, and volcanic eruptions, the nation's communications network required unusually high maintenance costs.[15] It was, moreover, a fragile system that, once constructed, required constant upkeep.

The wars of independence severely damaged agriculture, commerce, industry, and mining, as well as the nation's complex but delicate infrastructure. Lamentably, the most serious fighting occurred in central Mexico, the richest agricultural and mining area of the country. Rebels burned farms, killed livestock, wrecked mining equipment, and paralyzed commerce. Royalist forces retaliated with counter-terror, devastating regions which had capitulated to or supported the insurgents. The viceregal government lost control of most of the country to rebel bands or to royalist military leaders who acted without regard for law or the needs of the economy. By 1821, when Mexico achieved independence, the nation was in chaos and the economy in ruins.[16] Although it is impossible to assess the full impact of the struggle for independence, contemporaries attempted to calculate the magnitude of the carnage and destruction. José María Luis Mora believed that about 600,000 people—more than one-tenth of the population—perished from war, disease, and famine between 1810 and 1816, the period of heaviest fighting.[17] Quirós provides the best estimates of the losses caused by the war. He, like others, maintains that agriculture suffered great damage. But as he demonstrates, the most severe blow to the Mexican economy was the loss

TABLE V
Estimates of Damage Caused by Wars of Independence, 1810–1816*

Loss to Agriculture	70,000,000
Loss to Mining	20,000,000
Loss to Industry	11,818,000
Loss in Currency (mostly silver)	786,000,000

*In pesos.

Source: Calculated from José María Quirós, *Memoria de estatuto* (Veracruz, 1817).

of capital; money either fled the country or was withdrawn from circulation.

Why did Mexico not recover soon after independence? Why did it sink into fifty years of economic depression and political turmoil? The answer is both economic and psychological. The economy was in ruins as a result of the wars of independence and, especially, as a result of the post-independence political chaos. But in addition, Mexicans lost confidence in their country's institutions. They either exported their capital or withdrew it from circulation. This, along with the collapse of the nation's credit system, led to a massive contraction of investment. Although Mexico obtained foreign loans and investments in the post-independence period, they were insufficient to compensate for the great loss of national capital.

Contemporary observers provide us with graphic accounts of post-independence conditions. In 1822, Joel Poinsett, the first United States minister to Mexico, noted the destruction of many haciendas and the great financial loss such devastation represented to agriculturalists. He depicted San Felipe, Guanajuato, a once-prosperous farming and mining center, as representing

> *another example of the horrors of civil war. Scarcely a house was entire; and except for one church lately rebuilt, the town appeared to be in ruins. We stopped in the principal square, and passed through arches built of porphyry into a courtyard of a building which had once been magnificent; nothing but the porticos and the ground floor remain.*[18]

The English traveler G. F. Lyon described the situation on the road between the once-rich mining cities of San Luis Potosí and Zacatecas as follows:

> The prosperity of this place [an hacienda] is attributed to the owner having armed his people in defense of his property during the devastating Revolutionary War; and its contrast with Ranchos [middle sized farms] which we had passed on our day's ride was very striking. There we saw the houses roofless and in ruins blackened by fire, and had ridden over plains still bearing the faint trace of the plow; but the Rancheros who had tilled this ground had been murdered with their whole families during the war.[19]

All published travel accounts report similar devastation. Perhaps the great silver mining region of Guanajuato demonstrates most accurately post-war Mexico's changed conditions. During 1801–1809, its mines produced silver worth 47,000,000 pesos, but yielded only 22,000,000 in the following decade.[20] In 1820, the flooding of Valenciana, the greatest silver mine in the world, proved catastrophic because, as the Ayuntamiento observed,

> Valenciana, the incomparable Valenciana . . . the only mine that has for some time continued to support almost all our population, though with hardship, will be utterly stopped . . . It is believed that the remains of what used to be our numerous population will now flee the city to emigrate, to seek sustenance somewhere else, for here, when the mines and refineries do not function there is absolutely nothing to do. The prime harvests that the bounty of this year promises will not aid Guanajuato for there will be no one to buy and no money to buy it with.[21]

Apparently, the city council's assessment proved quite accurate because travelers subsequently described the city as desolate, filled with unemployed, poverty-stricken people who huddled in misery in the remains of ruined buildings.

Even the great metropolis, Mexico City, seems to have lost population. Many of those who remained suffered from unemployment or severe underemployment. Visitors left vivid accounts of these poor wretches, whom they called *léperos*, or lepers, because of their filthy, tattered clothes.[22] All reports indicate that the work force had severely contracted. Thousands of miners, textile workers, artisans, muleteers, carters, and other skilled workers lost their jobs.

The destruction of the silver mines during the wars of independence and the chaos that followed were, perhaps, the most important factors in Mexico's economic depression. The speedy rehabilitation of the mining sector would have immensely aided national recovery, but the problems associated with reviving the mines proved insurmountable. The combatants destroyed expensive machinery that was difficult to replace; equipment that escaped vandalism was often neglected, allowed to rust, or otherwise deteriorate. The fighting interdicted supplies required by the mining centers. Without those supplies, the mines could not function. They consumed thousands of hides, since leather was used to make many things that are today manufactured from rubber or plastic, such as impermeable containers, belts, and gaskets. The mines also used large quantities of other materials, such as grain to feed workers and draft animals; hemp for ropes, bags, and other equipment; carts and mules for transport; and cloth. The suspension of mining operations often resulted in severe damage to the mines themselves. Mexico's richest mines extracted ore from the world's deepest mine shafts. Left unattended, these deep tunnels rapidly flooded with ground water seepage, or, as in the case of Valenciana, heavy rains. Eventually, the flooding weakened the timbers and other supports, causing the tunnels to collapse. Once cave-ins occurred, it became tremendously expensive to reopen the mines.[23]

Two additional factors affected the recovery of the mines: mercury supplies and finances. Mexico's silver mines relied

An hacendado *and his wife receiving a report from their* mayordomo.

primarily on the patio or amalgamation process for separating silver from the ore. This technique required large quantities of mercury. At the onset of the nineteenth century, there were only three important sources of mercury: the Huancavelica mine in Peru, the Adria mine in present-day Yugoslavia, and the Almadén mine in Spain. The output of the Huancavelica mercury mine had declined and, after independence, could satisfy only Peruvian needs. International politics curtailed Mexican access to mercury from European mines: the Austrian empire, an ally of Spain, controlled Adria. Spain's Almadén mercury mine refused to supply Mexico until after 1838, when the two nations established diplomatic relations. Thus, while Mexican miners could purchase quicksilver through intermediaries, the supplies were never certain. The cost of mercury increased dramatically, not only because of its scarcity, but also because Spain had subsidized silver mining by providing mercury to Mexican miners at cost. In an independent Mexico, mine owners had to pay prevailing market prices for mercury.

Finances, however, were the greatest obstacle to the recovery of mining. In the colonial period, Mexican entrepreneurs had raised millions of pesos from local sources to finance mining operations. The war and the unstable conditions that followed destroyed the public confidence necessary for investment. Mexicans and foreigners alike agreed that the collapse of the country's investment and credit system prevented recovery.[24] Unable to raise the necessary quantities of money internally, Mexican miners formed joint stock companies to attract foreign capital to Mexico. The English invested heavily in silver mines and frequently became the major stockholders of Mexican mines. But the cost of rebuilding Mexican silver mines proved to be so great that the British silver mining ventures were bankrupt by the middle of the nineteenth century.[25] Mexicans subsequently benefitted from these investments; when mining recovered in the 1880s, nationals had regained control of the industry.

The textile industry, like silver mining, proved difficult to revive after independence. Woolen and cotton textile production had been the largest and most important manufacturing enterprise in colonial Mexico. *Obrajes*, large-scale factories employing several hundred workers, were common in central Mexico, principally Querétaro, Puebla, and Mexico City. Indian villages often engaged in large-scale textile production in community-run obrajes. There were also many individuals operating small firms with one or two looms. In the eighteenth century, these small enterprises manufactured more than one-third of New Spain's woolen cloth. The wars of independence and the chaos that followed crippled the industry: many obrajes were destroyed, and those which survived encountered difficulty in obtaining raw materials and distributing their finished products because transportation networks were disrupted. In addition, for a few years in the 1820s, Europeans flooded the Mexican market with cheap textiles, thus reducing the demand for local products.

After independence, the Mexican government tried to rehabilitate the textile industry by imposing high tariffs and by financing the modernization of the industry. Although tariff barriers substantially reduced the influx of foreign textiles, the Mexican factories recovered slowly. The greatest obstacle was the shortage of capital. To overcome this deficiency, the Mexican government founded a development bank, the Banco de Avío, in 1830 which, unfortunately, did not possess sufficient resources to stimulate a rapid recovery. Government reports indicate that by 1846, the Banco de Avío had contributed less than ten percent of the ten million pesos which industrialists had invested in the textile industry. Puebla was the principal beneficiary of this investment. The city was well located to benefit from the stimulus because of its proximity to the large Mexico City market and to the port of Veracruz, which facilitated the importation of equipment. By the mid-nineteenth century, textiles, primarily cotton, reemerged as an important industry in Puebla, but total Mexican production still did not equal the average of late colonial output until the 1880s.[26]

Agriculture, which employed the overwhelming majority of Mexicans, could not escape the dislocations that beset the industrial sector. Government reports, travel accounts, and private correspondence indicate the wretched condition of commercial agriculture. Small farmers appear to have suffered most. Many were driven from their lands, first by the war and then by the violence, political chaos, and economic decline that followed. Since small farmers were the backbone of Mexican agriculture, their plight had severe repercussions.[27] Farmers lost their markets when the mines collapsed and urban centers contracted. Many Indian villages, which had once produced for the market, withdrew into subsistence agriculture. In the colonial period, large numbers of Indian communities specialized in growing wheat for the urban markets or the mines; others devoted their efforts to raising mules for transport and for heavy work in mines and factories. In 1800, villages raised millions of mules; by 1850, the number had fallen to thousands. Depressed demand for agricultural products resulted in the abandonment of large tracts of land which formerly had been cultivated. Irrigation systems decayed, while livestock depleted the soil by overgrazing.

Mexico, City, and a few other large population centers, continued to demand agricultural products from the countryside, but after independence, they curtailed imports from distant regions; local production sufficed for their needs. Many large estates went bankrupt or were abandoned. As in the case of mining, Mexicans encouraged foreigners to invest in agriculture. Europeans purchased large estates in the early 1820s, but they also lost money. By the middle of the nineteenth century, European investors had relinquished their Mexican holdings. The small farmers, who managed to remain on the land, enjoyed a degree of prosperity because they could control their overhead more easily than the large hacendados.[28] Agriculture, like the rest of the economy, would not fully recover until the 1880s.

The slump in the mines limited the performance of Mexico's export sector in the post-independence period since silver remained the country's principal export; as mining declined, the nation's exports fell. Export substitution, given existing technology, was impossible; Mexico's high transportation costs prevented the export of bulky agricultural products at competitive prices. Because its excellent network of rivers permitted the shipment of these products at low cost, the United States, in contrast, exported a variety of agricultural commodities. Mexico's foreign trade stagnated at a time of massive and rapid expansion of world trade. By 1850, U.S. exports were twenty times greater than those of Mexico. Indeed, by the 1880s, when the silver mines recovered sufficiently to equal late colonial levels, the pattern of world trade had changed and new and significant silver producers had emerged, among them the United States. In 1800, Mexico had produced 75% of the world's silver; by 1880, its output represented less than 40%.[29]

Mexico required massive investment simply to restore it to the pre-independence level of production, but, unfortunately, the nation's credit system proved unequal to the task. Because Spain failed to develop modern financial institutions, such as banks and commercial houses, colonial Mexicans relied on two principal sources of credit: personal loans and the church. While personal loans from wealthy families or entrepreneurs were common throughout the colonial period, the church served as New Spain's principal banker. Convents, nunneries, schools, orphanages, and hospitals often received dowries, endowments, and bequests which they invested in order to earn regular income. Generally, religious corporations loaned these funds to property owners, who paid an annuity. Each diocese also had a *Juzgado de Testamentos, Capellanías, y Obras Pías* (Court of Testaments, Chantries, and Pious Works) which administered the endowments entrusted to the tribunal by the faithful. (A capellanía was a benefice for a chaplain who was required to say masses for the soul of the benefactor, and a pious work could be any sort of charity.) The juzgados invested these sums by lending primarily to land owners. As was the case with credit extended by other church bodies, the juzgados sought to earn a return of five to six percent on the capital so that the chaplain or the philanthropy would enjoy a regular income. Over the years, religious corporations invested vast sums of money in the economy of New Spain.[30]

Small farmers and Indian villagers who did not possess adequate collateral or were unwilling to mortgage their lands often turned to the *repartimiento de comercio*, an informal system through which provincial officials distributed seed, tools, and other agricultural necessities on credit. These magistrates often facilitated the purchase or sale of livestock, and marketed products for groups who might not have otherwise found outlets for their commodities. The officials were able to provide credit because they established commercial ties with wealthy entrepreneurs. The repartimiento system offered opportunities for abuse since magistrates sometimes used their authority to force Indian communities and small farmers to buy items they did not need or to sell their products at lower than market prices. Despite occasional irregularities, the repartimiento de comercio functioned reasonably well as a system of rural credit.[31]

Mexico's credit structure came under attack even before the wars of independence. Eighteenth century enlightened Spanish reformers criticized what they considered to be the evils of the repartimiento de comercio and the system of church credit. In the 1790s, they convinced the crown to abolish the repartimiento de comercio, contending that it exploited Indian communities. Then in 1804, the colonial credit structure suffered a crippling blow when the crown ordered the confiscation of church wealth to prosecute the war in Europe. Between 1804 and 1808, church bodies had to foreclose on loans totaling 44 million pesos, 12 million of which they remitted to Spain. The assaults on Mexico's credit structure debilitated the economy and fomented the discontent which eventually culminated in the movement for independence.[32]

While the wars of emancipation aggravated Mexico's already weakened credit system, the instability and chaos that followed engendered a severe loss of confidence. As a result, wealthy entrepreneurs refused to extend credit to individuals, preferring instead to lend for a short term, at exorbitant rates, to the government. The practice continued after 1821 because the national government could not raise sufficient revenue through taxation. The entrepreneurs-turned-loan sharks justified their actions, arguing that other investments were unsafe and that the high interest they demanded was reasonable because governments, which often failed to pay their debts, were poor credit risks. The nation's financial crisis worsened because religious corporations began to lend large sums only to individuals or groups who were pro-clerical. This policy seemed warranted, in their view, because Spanish reformers had expropriated church wealth at the end of the colonial period and liberal republican governments continued to threaten their holdings after independence.

As a result of these events, the credit system which had served New Spain well for nearly 300 years virtually ceased to function after independence. Mexico's government and entrepreneurs increasingly had to turn to foreign credit sources. Although foreigners, mostly the English, did invest large sums in Mexico, the amount did not satisfy the country's needs. Mexico did not develop an adequate modern banking and credit system until the 1880s.

The process of national recovery required more than sixty years. Unfortunately for Mexico, drastic changes transformed the world economic system during those decades. The Industrial Revolution altered the north Atlantic. In 1800, the United States was a second-rank agrarian nation while Western Europe was only beginning to industrialize. Many contemporaries, among them Alexander von Humboldt, believed not only that Mexico could compete successfully for economic hegemony, but that it would emerge as the colossus of the American continent.[33] No one had such illusions in 1880: the United States was an emerging industrial power; Western European industrial corporations and financial institutions had achieved such size and strength that nascent Mexican enterprises could not compete with them. After 1876, the leaders of a recently unified Mexico, therefore, decided to exchange economic independence for external assistance in industrial and financial development. Although this step led to rapid industrialization and modernization, it placed the control of Mexican development in the hands of foreigners. The violent Revolution of 1910 rejected that accommodation. Since 1910, Mexican governments have balanced the desire for national economic sovereignty with the need for foreign capital and technology. One can only speculate how Mexico might have developed without the nineteenth century crisis.

Muleteers in the high country.

Notes

1. This discussion is based on my work with Colin M. MacLachlan, *The Forging of the Cosmic Race: A Reinterpretation of Colonial Mexico* (Berkeley, 1980).

2. Henry G. Ward, *Mexico in 1827* 2d ed., 2 vols. (London, 1829), 1: 383.

3. David Brading has written extensively on mining. See: *Miners and Merchants in Bourbon Mexico, 1780–1810* (Cambridge, 1971); "La minería de la plata en el siglo XVIII: el caso de Bolaños," *Historia mexicana* 18 (1969): 317–333; "Mexican Silver in the 18th Century: The Revival of Zacatecas," *Hispanic American Historical Review* 53 (August, 1973): 389–414. See also Roberto Moreno, "Las instituciones de la industria minera novohispana," in Miguel León Portilla et. al., *La minería en México* (Mexico, 1978), pp. 69–164.

4. John H. Coatsworth, "Obstacles to Economic Growth in Nineteenth Century Mexico," *American Historical Review* 83 (February, 1978): 82.

5. There have been several attempts to calculate both the GNP and the per capita income of Mexico ca. 1800 from the data gathered by José María Quirós, *Memoria de estatuto* (Veracruz, 1817). See, for example, Fernando Rosenzweig Hernández, "La economía novo-hispana al comenzar el siglo XIX," *Ciencias políticas y sociales* 9 (July–Sept., 1963): 455–494; Doris M. Ladd, *The Mexican Nobility at Independence* (Austin, 1976), p. 26. Henry G. Aubrey, "The National Income of Mexico," *I.A.S.I. Estadística* (June, 1950), based his conclusion on Alexander von Humboldt, *Essai politique sur le royaume de la Nouvelle-Espagne*, 5 vols. (Paris, 1811). Clark W. Reynolds compared Aurbrey's and Rosenzweig's figures in "The Per Capital Income of New Spain Before Independence and After the Revolution," which is Appendix A of his book, *The Mexican Economy* (New Haven, 1970). John H. Coatsworth has recently reexamined New Spain's per capita income in his "Obstacles to Economic Growth." Unfortunately, he neither lists his sources for Mexico clearly nor does he explain his method.

Aside from minor errors of computation found in the figures originally published by Humboldt and Quirós, the major problem in calculating GNP in 1800 is establishing the correct size of New Spain's population. Most scholars generally accept six million as the size of Mexico's population ca. 1810. There are two problems with that figure. If one accepts the number, the subsequent population growth in the next four decades is so low as to be nonexistent. Such a phenomenon is not consistent with the facts. Also, the census of 1793 arrives at a much lower figure. That census, which was the only serious count obtained in the period under consideration, has always had its critics. Contemporaries, like José de Alzate, Alexander von Humboldt, Fernando Navarro y Noriega, Juan López Cancelada, and Tadeo Ortíz de Ayala, subjected the enumeration to criticism and raised the count substantially. Recently, critics have reviewed the census and given their own assessments; see, for example, Victoria Lerner, "La población de la Nueva España," *Historia mexicana* 28 (January–March, 1968): 327–346; Romeo Flores Caballero, *La contrarrevolución en la independencia* (Mexico, 1969), pp. 15–24; and Gonzalo Aguirre Beltrán, *La población negra de México*, 2d edition (Mexico, 1972), p. 230 and passim. I find Aguirre Beltrán's analysis the most searching and, in my view, the most nearly accurate. He concludes that the population of New Spain, exclusive of Cuba, Central America, and the Philippines, was approximately 3,799,561 people. Therefore, I have used 4,000,000 as the population of New Spain in 1800. Although this, in effect, raised my estimated per capita income, I am convinced it represents a sound estimate.

In comparing Mexican with United States and English per capita incomes, I have relied on Coatsworth where his figures do not conflict with mine because he has the best data for the other countries and for late periods of Mexican history. I have followed him in using 1950 dollars as a basis of comparison for per capita income calculations. But I have retained the original figures for GNP in 1800 to allow a direct comparison with the calculations made by Quirós and his contemporaries.

6. Aguirre Beltrán, *La población negra*, p. 230.

7. MacLachlan and Rodríguez, *The Forging of the Cosmic Race*, pp. 196–228.

8. The political history of post-independence Mexico remains confused. Among the best studies are: William S. Robertson, *Iturbide of Mexico* (Durham, 1952); Flores Caballero, *La contrarrevolución*; Jaime E. Rodríguez O., *The*

Emergence of Spanish America (Berkeley, 1975); Michael P. Costeloe, *La primera República Federal de México 1824-1835* (Mexico, 1975); Charles Macune, *El Estado de México y la federación mexicana* (Mexico, 1978); Fernando Díaz Díaz, *Caudillos y caciques* (Mexico, 1972); Moisés González Navarro, *Anatomía del poder en México* (Mexico, 1977).

9. Karl Marx in Marx and Engels, *Collected Works*, 16 vols. (New York, 1976), 8: 365-366. Marx also acknowledged that Mexicans in the conquered territories would lose their "independence" and suffer from discrimination but, in his view, that did not matter in comparison to the progress which the Americans would bring. Similarly, Frederick Engels declared: "In America we have witnessed the conquest of Mexico and have rejoiced at it . . . It is to the interest of its own development that Mexico will be placed under the tutelage of the United States." Marx and Engels, *Collected Works*, 6: 527. Although both men justified their views on the grounds that the United States was bringing capitalism to a feudal Mexico, it is clear that racist beliefs colored their analysis. In their works, Mexicans are described as "lazy," "decadent," and "degenerate," while Americans are called "energetic," "dynamic," and "progressive."

10. Jenaro González Reyna, *Riqueza minera y yacimientos minerales de México* (Mexico, 1947), p. 109.

11. Miguel Lerdo de Tejada, *El comercio exterior de México*, 2d edition, (Mexico, 1976), unnumbered tables; Inés Herrera Canales, *El comercio exterior de México, 1821-1875* (Mexico, 1977), pp. 58-75.

12. Coatsworth, "Obstacles to Economic Growth," p. 82 and passim

13. The contraction in commerce can be seen, for example, in the reduced activities of entrepreneurs such as the Sánchez Navarros; Charles H. Harris, *A Mexican Family Empire: The Latifundio of the Sanchez-Navarro Family, 1765-1867* (Austin, 1975); Díaz Díaz, *Caudillos y caciques* examines the role of regional bosses; and Harry Cross looks at "Living Standards in Rural Nineteenth Century Mexico: Zacatecas, 1820-1880," *Journal of Latin American Studies* 10 (May, 1978): 1-19.

14. On The best work on Mexican geography is Jorge L. Tamayo, *Geografía general de México*, 4 vols., 2d edition (Mexico, 1962). See also Claude Bataillon, *Las regiones geográficas en México* (Mexico, 1969).

15. On the problems of land transportation, see Salvador Ortíz Valades, *La arriería en México* (Mexico, 1929) and Peter Rees, *Transportes y comercio entre México y Veracruz, 1519-1910 (Mexico, 1976)*. David R. Ringrose presents an excellent analysis of similar problems in the mother country in his *Transportation and Economic Stagnation in Spain, 1750-1850* (Durham, 1970).

16. Flores Caballero, *La contrarrevolución*, 66-82. Christon Archer argues, in "The Royalist Army in New Spain: Civil-Military Relationships, 1810-1821" paper read at the Southern Historical Association meeting in Atlanta in 1979, that armed groups controlled most of the country during the wars of independence. In his view, the national government had lost all control in the provinces.

17. Hugh M. Hamill Jr. discusses Mora's estimates in "Was the Mexican Independence Movement a Revolution?" in *Dos revoluciones: México y los Estados Unidos* (Mexico, 1976), p. 43-61.

18. Joel R. Poinsett, *Notes on Mexico* (Philadelphia, 1824), pp. 178-179.

19. G. F. Lyon, *Journal of a Residence and Tour in the Republic of Mexico in 1826*, 2 vols. (London, 1828), 1: 192-193.

20. Lucas Alamán, *Historia de Méjico*, 5 vols. (Mexico, 1942), 2: 65-66.

21. Quoted in Ladd, *The Mexican Nobility*, p. 147.

22. For an excellent description of léperos, see Poinsett, *Notes on Mexico* and Fanny Calderón de la Barca, *Life in Mexico* (New York, 1966), pp. 91-92.

23. Ward, *Mexico*, 1: 398-400.

24. *Ibid.*; Quirós, *Memoria de estatuto*, pp. 24-29.

25. On British mining investments, see Newton R. Gilmore, "British Mining Ventures in Early National Mexico," (Ph.D. Dissertation, University of California, Berkeley, 1956) and Robert W. Randall, *Real del Monte: A British Mining Venture in Mexico* (Austin, 1972).

26. Robert A. Potash, *El Banco de Avío de México: el fomento de la industria, 1821-1846* (Mexico, 1959); Dawn Keremitsis, *La industria textil mexicana en el siglo XIX* (Mexico, 1973).

27. Ladd, *The Mexican Nobility*, pp. 139-140. On small farmers, see David Brading, *Haciendas and Ranchos in the Mexican Bajío: León, 1700-1860* (Cambridge, 1978).

28. The study of the 19th century Mexican agriculture remains in its infancy. Among the best works are: Brading, *Haciendas and Ranchos*; Eric van Young, "Rural Life in Eighteenth Century Mexico: The Guadalajara Region,

1675-1820" (Ph.D. Dissertation, University of California, Berkeley, 1978); the works of Jan Bazant, among them *Cinco haciendas mexicanas* (Mexico, 1975); and Harris, *A Mexican Family Empire*. Although not limited to agriculture, Harry E. Cross, "The Mining Economy of Zacatecas; Mexico in the Nineteenth Century" (Ph.D. Dissertation, University of California, Berkeley, 1976) provides much information on rural conditions.

29. Lerdo de Tejada, *El comercio exterior*; Herrera Canales, *El comercio exterior*, pp. 58-71; González Reyna, *Riqueza minera*, pp. 109-110.

30. The best study of the church as a banker is Michael P. Costeloe, *Church Wealth in Mexico* (Cambridge, 1976). Richard Lindley discusses the nature of personal credit and its decline in "Kinship and Credit in the Structure of Guadalajara's Oligarchy, 1800-1830" (Ph.D. Dissertation, University of Texas, Austin, 1975).

31. MacLachlan and Rodríguez, *The Forging of the Cosmic Race*, pp. 262-299.

32. Flores Caballero, *La contrarrevolución*, pp. 28-65; Asunción Lavrin, "The Execution of the Law of *Consolidación* in New Spain," *Hispanic American Historical Review* 52 (February, 1973): 27-49.

33. Humboldt, *Essai politique*.

Bibliography

Aguirre Beltrán, Gonzalo. *La población negra de México.* 2d. ed. México: Fondo de Cultura Económica, 1972.

Archer, Christon. "The Royalist Army in New Spain: Civil Military Relationships, 1810-1821." Paper read at the Southern Historical Association meeting in Atlanta in 1979.

Aubrey, Henry G. "The National Income of Mexico." *I.A.S.I. Estadística* (June, 1950): 185-198.

Bataillon, Claude. *Las regiones geográficas en México.* México: Siglo XXI, 1969.

Bazant, Jan. *Cinco haciendas mexicanas.* México: El Colegio de México, 1975.

Brading, David. "La minería de la plata en el siglo XVIII: el caso de Bolaños." *Historia mexicana* 18 (1969): 317-333.

———. *Miners and Merchants in Bourbon Mexico, 1780-1810.* Cambridge: Cambridge University Press, 1971.

———. "Mexican Silver in the 18th Century: The Revival of Zacatecas." *Hispanic American Historical Review* 53 (August, 1973): 387-414.

———. *Haciendas and Ranchos in the Mexican Bajío: León, 1700-1860.* Cambridge: Cambridge University Press, 1978.

Calderón de la Barca, Fanny. *Life in Mexico.* New York: Doubleday, 1966.

Coatsworth, John H. "Obstacles to Economic Growth in Nineteenth Century Mexico." *American Historical Review* 83 (February, 1978): 80-100.

Costeloe, Michael P. *La primera República Federal de México, 1824-1835.* México: Fondo de Cultura Económica, 1975.

Cross, Harry. "The Mining Economy of Zacatecas; Mexico in the Nineteenth Century." Ph.D. dissertation, University of California, Berkeley, 1976.

———. "Living Standards in Rural Nineteenth Century Mexico." *Journal of Latin American Studies* 10 (May, 1978): 1-19.

Díaz Díaz, Fernando. *Caudillos y caciques.* México: El Colegio de México, 1977.

Flores Caballero, Romeo. *La contrarrevolución en la independencia.* México: El Colegio de México, 1969.

Gilmore, Newton R. "British Mining Ventures in Early National Mexico." Ph.D. dissertation, University of California, Berkeley, 1956.

González Reyna, Jenaro. *Riqueza minera y yacimientos minerales en México.* México: Banco de México, 1947.

Harris, Charles H. *A Mexican Family Empire: The Latifundio of the Sanchez-Navarro Family, 1765-1867.* Austin: University of Texas Press, 1975.

Herrera Canales, Inés. *El comercio exterior de México, 1821-1875.* México: El Colegio de México, 1977.

Humboldt, Alexander von. *Essai politique sur le royaume de la Nouvelle-Espagne.* 5 vols. Paris: F. Schoell, 1811.

Keremitsis, Dawn. *La industria textil mexicana en el siglo XIX*. México: Secretaría de Educación Pública, 1973.

Ladd, Doris M. *The Mexican Nobility at Independence*. Austin: Institute of Latin American Studies, The University of Texas, 1976.

Lavrin, Asunción. "The Execution of the Law of Consolidation in New Spain." *Hispanic American Historical Review* 52 (February, 1973): 27–49.

Lerdo de Tejada, Miguel. *El comercio exterior de México*. 2d. ed. México: Banco Nacional de Comercio, 1976.

Lerner, Victoria. "La población de la Nueva España." *Historia mexicana* 28 (January–March, 1968): 327–346.

Lindley, Richard. "Kinship and Credit in the Structure of Guadalajara's Oligarchy, 1800–1830." Ph.D. dissertation, University of Texas, Austin, 1975.

Lyon, G. F. *Journal of a Residence and Tour in the Republic of Mexico*. 2 vols. London: J. Murray, 1828.

MacLachlan, Colin M., and Rodríguez O., Jaime E. *The Forging of the Cosmic Race: A Reinterpretation of Colonial Mexico*. Berkeley: University of California Press, 1980.

Macune, Charles. *El Estado de México y la federación mexicana*. México: Fondo de Cultura Económica, 1978.

Marx, Karl, and Engels, Frederick. *Collected Works*. 16 vols. New York: International Publishers, 1976.

México. Secretaría de Hacienda. *Memoria, 1823–1850*. (Title varies over the years).

Moreno de los Arcos, Roberto. "Las instituciones de la industria minera novohispana." In Miguel León Portilla et al. *La minería en México*. México: Universidad Nacional Autónoma de México, 1978. Pp. 68–164.

Ortíz Valades, Salvador. *La arriería en México*. México, 1929.

Poinsett, Joel R. *Notes on Mexico*. Philadelphia: H. C. Carey and I. Lea, 1824.

Potash, Robert. *El Banco de Avío de México: El fomento de la industria, 1821-1846*. México: Fondo de Cultura Económica, 1959.

Quirós, José María. *Memoria de estatuto*. Veracruz, 1817.

Randall, Robert W. *Real del Monte: A British Mining Venture in Mexico*. Austin: University of Texas Press, 1976.

Rees, Peter. *Transportes y comercio entre México y Veracruz*. México: Secretaría de Educación Pública, 1976.

Reynolds, Clark W. *The Mexican Economy: Twentieth-Century Structure and Growth*. New Haven: Yale University Press, 1970.

Ringrose, David. *Transportation and Economic Stagnation in Spain, 1750-1850*. Durham: Duke University Press, 1970.

Robertson, William S. *Iturbide of Mexico*. Durham: Duke University Press, 1952.

Rodríguez O., Jaime E. *The Emergence of Spanish America: Vicente Rocafuerte and Spanish Americanism, 1808-1832*. Berkeley: University of California Press, 1975.

Rosenzweig Hernández, Fernando. "La economía novohispana al comenzar el siglo XIX." *Ciencias políticas y sociales* 9 (July-Sept., 1963): 455-494.

Soetbeer, Adolf. *Edelmetall-produktion und werthverhältniss zwischen gold und silber*. Gotha. 1874.

Tamayo, Jorge L. *Geografía general de México*. 4 vols. 2d ed. Mexico, 1962.

Van Young, Eric. "Rural Life in Eighteenth Century Mexico: the Guadalajara Region, 1675-1820." Ph.D. dissertation, University of California, Berkeley, 1978.

Ward, Henry G. *Mexico in 1827*. 2 vols. 2d ed. London: Henry Colburn, 1829.